The Most Basic Arabic

Learn Arabic the Easy Way

James McGlasson & Dr. Ahmad Hamdy

Aim

This booklet is meant for those travelling to, moving to or living in the Middle East, and provides all the language you will need to get by while there. Please note that the "Arabic" referred to throughout this booklet is Egyptian Arabic, which is the most widely understood form of Arabic, even if it is not the native dialect of each area or country (there is a note on dialects towards the end of the book).

Introduction

It was decided not to include the Arabic script in this book, since the aim with this is to be able to communicate effectively with people orally. Therefore, the written Arabic is not given with each word or phrase because we thought it would confuse rather than aid most readers of this particular book.

The alphabet and written system is a whole subject of its own, and for those of you who wish to learn it and be able to use it, please check back to the MostBasicLanguages.com website because we will be producing a separate (cheap) book or booklet for this, which will go into detail on the Arabic alphabet and script.

Also, as you may realise from the title, a lot of the more advanced grammar will not be covered here – this book aims to teach the 'Arabic of the streets', meaning that there are a couple of things taught that are not officially correct, but this is the way most people actually use the language.

An equivalent example in English is 'each other'. This phrase (e.g. "We spoke to each other" should only really be used if more than two people are involved, and if it is just two people, we should really say "We spoke to one another"). However, the vast majority of English speakers use this 'incorrectly' by the rules of grammar, and therefore it is worth foreigners learning the incorrect usage if they are looking to communicate well in general conversation with the majority of the English-speaking population.

The same goes for Arabic, where there are many complex grammatical rules which the general population do not use. In this way, as mentioned above, this book aims to cover the basic 'Arabic of the streets' rather than necessarily all of the precisely correct grammar (although having said that, the vast majority of what is covered in the book is also grammatically correct).

There are some notes towards the back of the book, outlining a couple of these language points. For the purpose of being able to communicate effectively, what is presented in this book is more than sufficient.

How to use this booklet

On arrival and for your first couple of days in the Middle East, you will need 'The 10 Most Useful Phrases for a Newcomer'.

Then, with just the language in the rest of the booklet, you can easily survive in the area for anything from a week to several years.

The language is presented in both **English** in **Bold** and *Arabic* (written in the Roman script we are used to) in *Italics* with a guide to aid pronunciation [in square brackets].

The book is set up with the following structure and works through in an order designed to aid with learning the language building blocks step-by-step, as well as to keep the language separated into sections that are easy to refer back to later.

Basic Language Section
Pronunciation, basic pronouns, 'to be', basic verbs, 'to have', nouns and adjectives, questions, numbers and their uses.

Phrases Section
Basic conversation, in a taxi, in a bar or coffee shop, in a restaurant, in a shop, extra vocab (conjunctions & prepositions)

More Advanced Language
Verbs (grammar & more tenses), 'to be' (more tenses), more advanced language points.

Table of Contents

Phrases & Conversation

More Advanced Language

1. The 10 Most Useful Phrases for a Newcomer

1. **Hello**
Salaam alaykum   [sah-**laah'm** ah-lay-kuh'm]
OR:
Marhaban (informal)   [mah'r-hah-bah'n]

2. **Thank you**
Shukran   [shook-ran]

(You're welcome
Bekoll soror   [beh-koll soh-roar])

3. **Sorry / Excuse me**
Afwan   [ahf-wah'n]

4. **How much (is this)?**
Bikam (haza)?   [be-**kahm** hah-zah]

5. **I want this**   (can be used in a shop)
Oreedo haza   [oh-ree-doh hah-zah]

6. **Go to…**   (in a taxi)
Ezhab ela...   [eh'z-hahb eh-lah]
e.g. '*Ezhab ela al-matar*' – Go to the airport

7. **Do you speak English?**
Hal tatahaddath al-Englezia   [hal tah-tah-had-dath al-eng-leh-zee'ah]

8. **Goodbye**
Ma'a as-salama   [maah ass-sah-**laah**-mah]

9. **I don't understand**
Lam afham   [lam ahf-ham]

10. **Where is the toilet?**
Ayna al-hammam   [ay-nah al-ham-**ah'm**]

NB: The 2 words below indicate Male and Female, and are used to identify the men's and women's toilets.

رجال Male

سيدات Female

6

BASIC LANGUAGE

2. Pronunciation

For the most part, the pronunciation in this book will be quite straightforward, because the Arabic itself is transcribed in our alphabet, but there are some things to note with this, and Arabic also has various sounds that do not exist in English, which are given below.

It is mainly the vowels and a couple of sounds that have interesting differences, and you should take note where you see the following letters and letter groups (anything is not shown here, at least as far as this book goes, will be pronounced the same as the English letters given).

Vowels
a   Can either be like 'a' in 'father' or like 'a' in 'cat'
aa   Like 'a' in father' or 'a' in 'cat', but more drawn out
a'a   Both *a*'s are heard, so [ah'ah]
e   'e' in 'eh' or 'bed'
ee   Can be 'ay' in 'day' or 'ee' in 'keep'
i   'ee' in 'keep', but not as drawn out
o   'oh', or 'oo' if at the end of the word

Consonants

kh   This is like the [ch] in the Scottish word 'loch' (like a strong 'H' – the correct position for your mouth is as if you're saying 'k' [k'uh] and then breathing through it strongly). This is shown as [KH] in the pronunciation guide to indicate its force.

gh   This sound is really the above sound ('kh') but voiced. It sounds a bit like a strong 'rolled R'. This is shown as [RR] in the pronunciation guide.

zh   In this book, this is 2 separate sounds, so simply [z] then [h]. Just mentioned here, in case it is tempting to read this any other way.

The sounds for the rest of the pronunciation in this guide are the same as English.

3. Pronouns

3a. General

I/me, you, he/she, we/us, they/them, my/mine, your/yours etc.

Pronouns in Arabic are a little different to those in English and we can learn them in 3 simple stages, namely Subject (I, you, he, she etc), Object (me, you, him, her etc), and Possessive (my, your, his, her etc).

3b. Subject Pronouns (I, you, he, she, we, they)

Subject pronouns (I, you, he / she, we, they) have direct equivalents in Arabic and are used in a similar way.

One thing to note in Arabic, is that there are two words to say 'you' (singular), depending on whether you are talking to a male or to a female. So, there is a male / female distinction with 'he / she', just as in English, but also with 'you' (to a male) and 'you' (to a female), as you will see below.

Another difference in Arabic is that there is no separate word for 'it'. As you will see in the 'Nouns' section of the book, Arabic nouns have genders, like in French and many European languages – however, Arabic genders are easier to identify and hence to learn than in European languages. This will be covered later, but for now, we just need to know that, to say 'it' in Arabic, we just use 'he' and 'she', depending on the noun – e.g. **car** is feminine, so we would say '**She**'s fast.' instead of 'It's fast.'

The list of pronouns below has been ordered in the simplest way to learn and remember in Arabic – you will see why, if you look at the similarities between certain pronouns:

1st Person singular and plural – I, We
2nd Person singular and plural – You (m.sg.), You (f.sg.), You (plural)
3rd Person singular and plural – He, She, They

1st Person
I *Ana* [ah-nah]
We *Nahnu* [nah-noo]

2nd Person
You (singular m.) *Anta* [an-tah]
You (singular f.) *Anti* [an-tee]
You (plural) *Antum* [an-tuh'm]

3rd Person
He, It (m. nouns) *Howa* [hoh-wah]
She, It (f. nouns) *Heya* [hey'ah]
They *Hum* [huh'm]

Examples:

I am English (for males)
Ana Englezy [ah-nah eng-gleh-zee]

I am English (for females)
Ana Englezyyah [ah-nah eng-gleh-zeh-yah]

You are Egyptian (for males)
Anta Masry [an-tah mass-ree]

You are Egyptian (for females)
Anti Masryyah [an-tee mass-reh-yah]

He is American
Howa Amreky [hoh-wah ah'm-reh-kee]

She is American
Heya Amrekyyah [hey'ah ah'm-reh-keh'yah]

We live in Cairo
Nahnu na'eesh fi al-qahirah [nah-noo nah-eh'sh fee al-kah-hear'ah]

In these examples above, note that the verb ('to be') has been omitted. Briefly, this is because it is not necessary to say the present tense of 'to be' – 'am', 'is', 'are', as will be discussed in a later chapter on the verb 'to be'.

For example, "He is American" translates to Arabic as "He American", and so on. With other verbs (i.e. not 'to be'), e.g. "We live in Cairo", the verb is stated just as you would expect.

3c. Object Pronouns (me, you, him, her, us, them)

In both Arabic and English, while subject pronouns come before the verb (**he** sees), object pronouns come after the verb (I see **him**).

In Arabic, however, the pronouns themselves are actually attached on to the end of the verb or preposition, making one new word (this is very straightforward and would simply amount to saying, in English, things like "I **seehim**" or "He **likesthem**" or "It is **forher**" with the pronoun being joined to the verb or preposition).

In addition to having male and female singular words for 'you' (as we have already seen), there is one more thing to note with object pronouns – that there are two words for 'me', which are shown in the table below. It is just that 'me' after verbs (e.g. 'he sees me') is slightly different to 'me' when it comes after prepositions (e.g. 'for me', 'to me' etc).

1st Person
Me (after verbs)   *-nee*   [knee]
Me (after prepositions)   *-ee/-y* (sometimes '*-yee*' for pronunciation)
Us   *-na*   [nah]

2nd Person
You (singular m.)   *-ka*   [kah]
You (singular f.)   *-ke*   [keh]
You (plural)   *-kum*   [kuh'm]

3rd Person
Him, It (m.)   *-hu*   [hoo]
Her, It (f.)   *-ha*   [hah]
Them   *-hum*   [huh'm]

Examples

Note how the object pronouns in the list above are actually joined to the end of the verb or preposition.

He goes with me ('me' after a preposition)
*Howa yazhab ma'**yee*** [hoh-wah **yah'z**-hah'b mah'yee]
('*ma*' = with)

She sees me ('me' after a verb)
*Heya tara**nee*** [hey'ah tah-rah-nee]
('*Heya tara*' = she sees)

I see him
*Ana ara**ho*** [ah-nah ah-rah-hoo]

They see us
*Hum yaroo**na*** [huh'm yah-roo-nah]

We see them
*Nahnu nara**hum*** [nah-noo nah-rah-huh'm]

11

3d. Possessive (my, your, his, her, our, their)

In English, we use possessive pronouns before the noun (e.g. **my** car).

In Arabic, however, there is almost no difference between the object pronouns shown above and the possessive pronouns. There is nothing new to learn because the list is exactly the same as the object pronouns (i.e. 'him' is the same word as 'his' in Arabic, and 'us' = 'our' etc), with just **one exception**.

The one exception is that you will have seen above that there are two words for 'me' in Arabic. This is not the case for 'my', and there is simply one word '-ee' for this.

Just like the object pronouns are joined to the end of the verb, as we have seen, possessive pronouns are joined to the end of the noun they refer to.

The possessive pronouns in Arabic are as follows (as already stated, the list is the same as before with the exception of 'my'):

1st Person
My -ee / -y (sometimes written as '-yee') [ee / yee]
Our -na [nah]

2nd Person
Your (singular m.) -ka [kah]
Your (singular f.) -ke [keh]
Your (plural) -kum [kuh'm]

3rd Person
His -hu [hoo]
Her -ha [hah]
Their -hum [huh'm]

Note that feminine nouns which end in '-ah' change their ending to '-at' before adding these, to make pronunciation slightly easier.

Examples:

My child is here
Tef**lee** hona (child: Tefl)
[teh-flee hoh-nah]

This is our friend
Haza sadeko**na** (friend: Sadeek)
[**hah**-zah sah-deh-koh-nah]

Her car is red
Sayyarat-__ha__ hamra (car: *Sayyarah*)
[sigh-yah-rah't-hah hah'm-rah]

3e. PRONOUNS SUMMARY

Subject:
I, we: *Ana, Nahnu*
You (male, female, plural): *Anta, Anti, Antum*
He, she, they: *Howa, Heya, Hum*

Object:
Me, us: *-nee/-ee, na*
You (male, female, plural): *-ka, -ke, -kum*
Him, her, them: *-hu, -ha, -hum*

Possessive:
My, our: *-ee, -na*
Your (male, female, plural): *-ka, -ke, -kum*
His, her, their: *-hu, -ha, -hum*

4. The Verb 'To Be' (Part 1)

Before looking at the other verbs, it is useful to cover the verb 'to be', which is the exception to the general verb rules. This should be familiar to us, because 'to be' is an exception in most ways in English as well. All verbs except 'to be' follow the same pattern as each other in Arabic`, which makes things easier for us as learners when compared with other languages.

So in Arabic, we will learn how to use the verb 'to be' first, and then we will cover the other verbs.

Present Tense of 'to be' (am, is, are)

The present tense of 'to be' is where the biggest difference lies, being simply that 'to be' is completely omitted in the present tense.

This just means that any time we would say '**am**', '**is**' or '**are**', we do not need to state the verb. So in English we say, for example, "I **am** a teacher." and "The children **are** late." In Arabic, these sentences become "I teacher." and "The children late." As you can imagine, this actually makes it easier rather than harder when speaking basic Arabic sentences.

Note that this only goes for the present tense of the verb 'to be' (no other verbs). For every other tense (I was / wasn't, we were / weren't, he will be / won't be etc), we state the verb as normal. This also doesn't go for negative sentences, where there is a verb form to include.

Although you will rarely need the present tense of 'to be' for 'basic Arabic', the forms are included on the next page, because they are needed to be able to form the future tense, which will be covered later, in the Verbs (Part 1) chapter on page 18 but it is just a case of adding '*sa-*' before the verb to mean 'will'. These forms are also used for other tenses, which we will see in Verbs (Part 2) on page 65.

To be *Yakon* [yah-kohn]

1st Person
I am *Ana Akon* [ah-kohn]
We are *Nahnu Nakon* [nah-kohn]

2nd Person
You (m.) are *Anta Takon* [tah-kohn]
You (f.) are *Anti Takooneen* [tah-koo-neen]
You (pl.) are *Antum Takoonoon* [tah-koo-noon]

3rd Person
He is *Howa Yakon* [yah-kohn]
She is *Heya Takon* [tah-kohn]
They are *Hum Yakoonoon* [yah-koo-noon]

Examples in the Present Tense
(Note that the verb 'to be' is omitted)

The car is fast ("The car fast")
Al-sayyarah sareeha [al-sigh-yah-rah sah-ree-hah]

We are happy ("We happy")
Nahnu soadaa [nah-noo soh'ah-daah]

Negative Present Tense of 'To Be' (am not, isn't, aren't)

As stated above, the present tense of 'to be' is simply omitted in positive sentences. If the sentence is negative, then while the verb itself is still omitted, there is another word (with various endings) we need to include for 'not', which is more useful to think of as 'isn't' / 'aren't' for our purposes of getting to grips with the language.

You will see later that negatives for the present of 'to be' are expressed differently to other verbs, which you can think of as somewhat similar to English – the negative of 'to be' in English is 'am not' / 'isn't' / 'aren't', while for all other verbs, we use 'doesn't' / 'don't' + verb (e.g. "I don't know"), so when we learn how to use the verbs later, we will learn the negative as meaning 'don't' / 'doesn't'. For this negative, however, we will consider it like 'am not' / 'isn't' / 'aren't'.

15

'am not' / 'isn't' / 'aren't'

To say '**am not**', '**isn't**' or '**aren't**' (i.e. the negative of 'to be' in the present), the verb 'to be' itself is dropped, but the negative word '*laysa*' is stated. '*Laysa*' changes with each pronoun as follows:

I'm not   *Ana Lastoo*   [lass-too]
We're not   *Nahnu Lasna*   [lass-nah]

You (m.) are not   *Anta Lasta*   [lass-tah]
You (f.) are not   *Anti Lasti*   [lass-tee]
You (pl.) are not   *Antum Lastum*   [lass-tuh'm]

He isn't   *Howa Laysa*   [lay-sah]
She isn't   *Heya Laysat*   [lay-saht]
They aren't   *Hum Laysoo*   [lay-soo]

Examples

The weather is fine
('**is**' will be dropped in Arabic, so literally, '**The weather fine**')
Al-jaw ~~yakon~~ saho ('*yakon*' means 'is').
> *Al-jaw saho*   [al-jow sah-hoh]

The weather isn't fine
(For negatives, we do say 'isn't' which, in this case, is '*laysa*'.
Al-jaw laysa saho   [al-jow lay-sah sah-hoh]

The car is fast
Al-sayyarah ~~takon~~ sareeha
> *Al-sayyarah sareeha*   [al-sigh-yah-rah sah-ree-hah]

The car isn't fast
Al-sayyarah laysat sareeha   [al-sigh-yah-rah lay-sat sah-ree-hah]

We are happy
Nahnu ~~nakon~~ soadaa
> *Nahnu soadaa*   [nah-noo soh'ah-daah]

We're not happy
Nahnu lasna soadaa   [nah-noo lass-nah soh'ah-daah]

Easy Practice

See if you can make the following sentences from the rules above:

1. **He is not happy.**
2. **I am a student.** ('student' = *taleb (m.)* or *talebah (f.)*)
3. **They are here.** ('here' = *hona*)
4. **They aren't here.**

5. Verbs (Part 1): Present & Future Tenses

5a. General

Verbs in Arabic can seem a little complex, but once you get your head around a few key differences, you will find they are easy enough to learn to use.

Key Things to Note:

- Arabic verbs don't only change their endings (like 'go', 'goes', but can also change their beginnings). Once learned, however, the same changes go for all Arabic verbs, so it is a case where a little effort at the start goes a long way. So it is definitely worth spending a bit of time with this chapter and familiarizing yourself with the verb forms, and you will find them easy to use in the future (you can also always refer back to this chapter).

- The first 2 verb tenses, which will be covered in this chapter and are the easiest to learn, are the Present and Future tenses. Later, in the Verbs (Part 2) chapter, you will also see the Simple Past, Past Continuous and Giving Orders.

- To make statements into questions in Arabic, all you need to do is say the statement with a rising (questioning) tone, and you can add the optional word '*hal*' before the statement.

E.g. **You see her** *Anta taraha* [an-tah tah-rah-hah]
Do you see her? *Anta taraha?* [an-tah tah-rah-hah?]
Do you see her? *Hal anta taraha?* [an-tah tah-rah-hah?]

5b. Present Tense

First, let's look at the present tense. In Arabic, the present tense of the verbs begins with '*Y-*' (e.g. 'to see' = '*Yara*', 'to go' = '*Yazhab*').

In most European languages, verbs change their endings according to the person (I, you, we etc) and the tense (past, present etc). In Arabic, it is both the beginning and the ending of the verbs that change according to these things.

Learning this is not as challenging as it sounds though since, as already mentioned, all verbs change in the same way – this means that once you know how one verb works, you know how they all work.

Now, let's demonstrate this by looking at one specific verb, '**to see**' (*Yara*), while remembering that this goes for all verbs. The verb forms in the present are as follows:

To See *Yara* [yah-rah]

I see *Ana Ara* [ah-rah]
We see *Nahnu Nara* [nah-rah]

You (m.) see *Anta Tara* [tah-rah]
You (f.) see *Anti Tareen* [tah-reen]
You (pl.) see *Antum Taroon* [tah-roon]

He sees *Howa Yara* [yah-rah]
She sees *Heya Tara* [tah-rah]
They see *Hum Yaroon* [yah-roon]

Negative for Present Tense (don't, doesn't)

Forming the negative in the present is very simple – just like in English, where we add 'don't' or 'doesn't' before the verb, in Arabic there is a similar word added before the verb. This word is '*La*' [lah].

Examples
(Just note the addition of the word '*La*' before the verb).

I play football *Ana ala'ab koarata alkadam*
I don't play football *Ana la ala'ab koarata alkadam*
[ah-nah (lah) ah-laah'b kaw-rah-tah al-kah-dah'm]

She sees me *Heya taranee* [hey'ah tah-rah-nee]
She doesn't see me *Heya la taranee* [hey'ah lah tah-rah-nee]

And so on…

5c. Future Tense

The future tense in English is probably the easiest tense to learn, because we basically just add the word 'will' before the verb ("I will go" etc). This is also the case in Arabic – it just involves adding the word '*Sa-*' or '*Sawfa-*'. There is no difference between these two, and you are free to choose either one. Note that in Arabic, the verb is conjugated with the same forms as given in the present tense, so it is '*Sa-*' or '*Sawfa-*' + Present Tense.

To See – *Yara* [yah-rah]

I will see *Ana Sa-Ara* [sah ah-rah]
We will see *Nahnu Sa-Nara* [sah nah-rah]

You (m.) will see *Anta Sa-Tara* [sah tah-rah]
You (f.) will see *Anti Sa-Tareen* [sah tah-reen]
You (pl.) will see *Antum Sa-Taroon* [sah tah-roon]

He will see *Howa Sa-Yara* [sah yah-rah]
She will see *Heya Sa-Tara* [sah tah-rah]
They will see *Hum Sa-Yaroon* [sah yah-roon]

Negative for the Future Tense
Just like for the present, we just need to add one word for the negative in the future. It is easiest to remember this word as being equivalent to '**won't**' in English.

Won't = *Lan* [lan]
(You will notice that the present and future negatives are almost the same – just add '*la*' for the present and '*lan*' for the future).

Example

I will play football
Ana sa-ala'ab koarata alkadam
[ah-nah sah-ah-laah'b kaw-rah-tah al-kah-dah'm]

I won't play football
Ana lan ala'ab koarata alkadam
[ah-nah lan ah-laah'b kaw-rah-tah al-kah-dah'm]

5d. Some Common Verbs

Arrive   *Yasel*   [yah-sel]

Come   *Ya'ate*   [yah'ah'teh]

Cook   *Yatbokh*   [yat-boH]

Do   *Yafaal*   [yah-faah'l]

Drink   *Yashrab*   [yah-shrab]

Eat   *Ya'akol*   [yah'ah-kol]

Get   *Yohder*   [yoh'dare]

Give   *Yoote*   [yoh'oh-teh]

Have (see chapter 8)   *Eind*   [eye'nd]

Go (to)   *Yazhab (ela)*   [yah'z-hah'b eh-lah]

Like, love   *Yohebb*   [yaw-heb]

Look   *Yanzor*   [yan-zor]

Play   *Yala'ab*   [yah-laah'b]

See   *Yara*   [yah-rah]

Speak   *Yatakallam*   [yah-tah-kal-lam]

Want   *Yoreed*   [yaw-reed]

Watch   *Yoshahed*   [yaw-shah-hed]

5e. VERBS 1 SUMMARY

Present Tense:
Begins with *Y-*, e.g. *Yazhab*
Ana: Minus 'Y-'
Nahnu: Minus 'Y-' Plus N-'

Anta: Minus 'Y-' Plus 'T-'
Anti: Minus 'Y-' Plus 'T-' Plus '-een'
Antum: Minus 'Y-' Plus 'T-' Plus '-oon'

Howa: No change
Heya: Minus 'Y-' Plus 'T-'
Hum: Plus '-oon'

Don't / Doesn't:
'*La*' before the verb

Future Tense:
'**Will**' = '*Sa-*' + Present Tense
'**Won't** = '*Lan*' + Present Tense

Practice

Make the following sentences from the list of verbs and summary given above (review the chapter if you have need to):

1. **I don't drink coffee.** (coffee = *Al-kahwa*)
2. **You (m.) will see him.**
3. **They will come.**
4. **She won't come.**
5. **We play football.** (football = *koarata alkadam*)
6. **She won't want it.**

Answers

1. **I don't drink coffee**.
Ana la ashrab al-kahwa   [ah-nah lah ash-rah'b al-kah-h'wah]

2. **You (m.) will see him.**
Anta sa-tara-hu   [an-tah sah-tah-rah-hoo]

3. **They will come.**
Hum sa-ya'atoon   [huh'm sah-yah'ah-toon]

4. **She won't come.**
Heya lan ta'ate   [hey'ah lan tah'ah-teh]

5. **We play football.** (football = *al-koarata alkadam*)
Nahnu nala'ab al-koarata alkadam
[nah-noo nah-laah'b al-koar-ah-tah al-kah-dam]

6. **She won't want this.** (this = *haza*)
Heya lan toreed haza   [hey'ah lan taw-reed hah-zah]

6. The Verb 'To Have'

The verb 'to have' in Arabic is different from all the other verbs – it is not actually a verb at all. The word '*eind*' is stated before the noun, and the pronoun endings for each person are added to the word ('*-ee/-y*', '*-na*', '*-ka*', '*-ke*', '*-kum*', '*-hu*', '*-ha*', '*-hum*').

have   *eind*   [eye'nd]

You don't need to add the initial pronouns (i.e. for '**I/you/we** etc have') since the pronouns are added in the endings instead. You can consider it something like 'belongs to me/you/him/her' etc, although it is not a direct equivalent and comes before the noun in Arabic.

I have   *eindee*   [eye'n-dee]
We have   *einduna*   [eye'n-duh-nah]

2nd Person
You (singular m.)   *einduka*   [eye'n-duh-kah]
You (singular f.)   *einduke*   [eye'n-duh-keh]
You (plural)   *eindukum*   [eye'n-duh-kuh'm]

3rd Person
Him, It (m.)   *einduhu*   [eye'n-duh-hoo]
Her, It (f.)   *einduha*   [eye'n-duh-hah]
Them   *einduhum*   [eye'n-duh-huh'm]

I have a car   *Eindee sayyarah*   [eye'n-dee sigh-yah-rah]

Do you have a house?   *Hal einduka manzel?*   [hal eye'n-duh-kah man-zel]

She has a bike   *Einduha darrajah*   [eye'n-duh-hah da-Rah-jah]

We have a shop   *Einduna mahal*   [eye'n-duh-nah mah-hal]

7. Nouns

7a. General

There are 3 major differences with nouns in Arabic compared to English.

- **Articles:** Arabic has a definite article, '**the**', but it has no indefinite article, '**a**' or '**an**'.
- **Genders:** Nouns have genders, meaning that nouns are either **masculine** or **feminine**, just like in French (though easier to identify which).
- **Plural:** While we just add an 's' to indicate plural for most nouns in English, in Arabic, plurals vary depending on the noun. Arabic also has a specific way to say '2 of something' (i.e. they have singular, dual and plural), and use the plural form for 3 or more of something.

The sections below will explain these in more detail.

7b. Articles

There are two big things to know about articles in Arabic. Firstly, even though Arabic nouns have genders, there is only one word for '**the**' (this means that it is not as complicated as in some European languages). Secondly, there is no indefinite article ('**a / an**'), which also makes things easier on us as learners.

The Arabic word for '**the**' is '*Al*'. This word is attached to the beginning of the noun, and goes for both singular and plural (there is a more advanced grammar point regarding this in the advanced language points (Adv. Lang.1 on page 64), but for basic Arabic, this will suffice). Also, as you will see in the Adjectives chapter, when '**the**' is added to the noun, it is also added to the adjective.

For example,
Car = *Sayyarah*   **The car** = *Al-Sayyarah*
Cars = *Sayyarat*   **The cars** = *Al-Sayyarat*
House = *Manzel*   **The house** = *Al-Manzel*
Houses = *Manazel*   **The houses** = *Al-Manazel*

As already stated, there is no indefinite article. This means that to say '**a car**' is the same as just saying '**car**', and '**a house**' is the same as '**house**'.

For example,
Car = *Sayyarah*   **A car** = *Sayyarah*   [sigh-yah-rah]
House = *Manzel*   **A house** = *Manzel*   [man-zel]

This also means that if you see a noun with *Al-* attached, it means '**the...**' and if there is no article, it means '**a / an**'.

7c. Genders

We have already said that there are 2 genders in Arabic, 'masculine' and 'feminine', and every noun is considered to be one or the other. The good thing about Arabic is that this is not as difficult to learn as in some other languages because it is normally **easy to identify feminine nouns** by the following general rules:

- Almost all nouns which **end in '*-ah*'** are feminine.
- Any noun which **refers to a female person** is also feminine, for obvious reasons.
- Then there are a relatively small number of feminine nouns, where the gender can be learned when the noun is learned.

Some examples of feminine nouns are:
Car   *sayyarah*   (ends in an 'ah')
Ruler   *mestarah*   (ends in an 'ah')
Aunt   *khalah* (maternal aunt) or *ammah* (paternal aunt)
Girl   *bent* (although it doesn't end with '*-ah*' it refers to a female person)

Masculine nouns comprise most of the nouns which **do not**:
- end in '-ah'
- refer to a female person

Some examples of masculine nouns:
Bed   *sareer*   [sah-rear]
Phone   *hatef*   [hah-tef]
Door   *bab*   [bah'b]
Shop   *mahal*   [mah-hal]

So now we know we have the two genders, let's look at what difference it makes as far as we are concerned when speaking.

- The gender does not change anything regarding '**the**' ('*Al*') or '**a**' (nothing), which always remain the same.

- Adjectives, which we will look at in the next chapter, do change their form depending on the gender.

- There is no word for '**it**' in Arabic, so we say '**he**' or '**she**' instead, depending on the gender (e.g. **car** is feminine so we say '**she**', while **phone** is masculine, so we would say '**he**' for this, and so on).

- When using words such as 'this' and 'that', there is also a masculine and feminine forms, which we will see later.

- The verb form will also change, as we have already learned, depending on whether it is 'he' or 'she' (see the 'he/she' forms in the verbs chapter if you need a reminder).

7d. Plural

Plurals in Arabic can be complicated, so the easiest way to learn them is to learn the plural for each word as you learn the word itself. This book has been designed to aid with this, and you will notice that each noun is given with its plural. As you gain experience in Arabic, you will find that you develop a 'feeling' or a 'sense' of what the plural of a noun is going to be, and that is when it becomes easier. But the way to get there in the beginning is just to learn the plural as you learn each noun.

In Arabic, the plural is used when talking about 3 or more of something. There is a special way to say '2 of something', which simply involves adding '-an' to the end of the noun. So, for example:

(a) car   *sayyarah*   [sigh-yah-rah]
2 cars   *sayyaratan*   [sigh-yah-rah-tah'n]
3 or more cars   *sayyarat*   [sigh-yah-rah't]

Please see the Stating How Many section on page 42 for more detailed notes and examples.

Pluralising feminine nouns is very easy. The plural of almost all feminine nouns is '-at'. The feminine nouns which end in '-ah', change to '-at', while other feminine nouns simply add '-at' [ah't].

'Woman' and 'girl' are two of the very rare exceptions to this rule:
Woman – *emra'ah*   [em-rah-ah]
Women – *nisa'a*   [nee-saah]

Girl – *bent*   [bent]
Girls – *banat* (3 or more girls)   [bah-nah't]

But other than that, it is very simple:

Lady – *sayyidah*   [sigh-yid-ah]
Ladies – *sayyidat* (3 or more)   [sigh-yid-ah't]

27

Car – *sayyarah*   [sigh-yah-rah]
Cars – *sayyarat* (3 or more)   [sigh-yah-rah't]

Female student – *talebah*   [tah-leh-bah]
Female students – *talebat* (3 or more)   [tah-leh-bah't]

Again, note that to say 2 of any of the above, '-*an*' is added to the end (e.g. *sayyidatan, sayyaratan*), as will be described in the Stating How Many section.

For masculine nouns, the plurals are a bit more complicated and take a bit more learning, but for the purposes of the book, and getting by, it will be much easier to learn the plurals with the nouns themselves. (The plural is included in brackets / parentheses after each noun).

7e. Some Common Nouns

Note that the nouns are given in the singular with plural in (brackets) / (parentheses).

People

Man   *rajol (rejal)*   [rah-jol / reh-jah'l]
Woman   *emra'ah (nisa'a)*   [em-rah-ah / nee-saah]
Boy   *walad (awlad)*   [wah-lad / ow-lad]
Girl   *bent (banat)*   [bent / bah-nat]

Friend (m.)   *sadeek (asdekaa)*   [sah-deek / **ass**-dek-aah]
Friend (f.)   *sadeekah (sadeekat)*   [sah-dee-kah / sah-dee-kah't]
 (My friend = *Sadeeky (m. friend), Sadeekaty (f. friend)*)

Boyfriend   *habib (ahbeb)*   [hah-beeb / ah-beb]
Girlfriend   *habibah (habibat)*   [hah-bee-bah / hah-bee-bah't]

Husband   *zawj*   [zow'dge]
Wife   *zawjat*   [zow'jah't]

Police   *shortah*   [sure-tah]
Policeman   *shorty (no plural)*   [sure-tee]
Teacher (m.)   *mudarris (mudarrisoon)*   [moo-**dah**-riss / -iss-oon]
Teacher   *mudarrisah (mudarrisat)*   [moo-**dah**-riss-ah / -iss-ah't]
Student (m.)   *taleb (taleban)*   [taah-leb / taah-leh-ban]
Student (f.)   *talebah (talebat)*   [taah-leh-bah / taah-leh-bah't]

Places

Home   *bayt / manzel*   [bait / man-zel]
 (I go home = *Ana azhab ela bayt / manzel*)

Airport   *matar (f., -at)*   [mah-**tahrr**]

Hotel   *hotel / fondok (fanadek)*   [foon-dook]
 (My hotel is on Talaat Harb – *Fondoky fi Talaat Harb*)

Restaurant   *mata'am (mata'em)*   [mah-taah'm / mah-tah-eh'm]
Shop   *mahall (f., mahallat)*   [mah-hah'll / -hah-lah't]
School   *madrasah (f., madares)*   [mah-drass-ah / mah-dah-ress]
Park   *hadeekah (f., hada'ek)*   [hah-dee-kah / hah-dah-eh'k]
Bathroom/Toilet   *hammam (m., hammamat)*   [hah-mah'm / -ah't]

Transport

Car *sayyarah (sayyarat)* [sigh-yah-rah / sigh-yah-rah't]
Bicycle *darrajah (darrajat)* [dahr-rah-jah / dahr-rah-jah't]
Bus *bus (bas'at)* [bus / bus-ah't]
Taxi *taxi* [taxi]
Train *ketar (ketarat)* [keh-tar / keh-tar-ah't]
Subway, metro *metro al-anfak* [metro al-an-fah'k]
Train station *mahattat ketar* [mah-hat-tat keh-tar]
  (I'm at the train station – *Ana fi Mahattat al-ketar)*

8. Adjectives

8a. General

For anyone who has learned French, Spanish or Italian, using adjectives in Arabic will come easily because they are used in the same way. For English-speakers, there are a few things to learn.

1. The <u>first difference</u> is that adjectives come before the noun in English but **after the noun in Arabic**, so "**big house**" in English becomes "**house big**" in Arabic. This is, of course, pretty simple once you know it.

2. The <u>second difference</u> from English is that, as we have seen that nouns in Arabic are either masculine of feminine, adjectives also change their form depending on whether the noun is masculine or feminine, as well as if it is singular or plural.

This is not too tough, because most adjectives just add '-*ah*' for feminine, and '-*oon*' for the plural, although there are some exceptions (e.g. big – *kibir, kibar (pl.)*.

3. The <u>third difference</u> is to do with the articles ('a' and 'the'). As we have already seen, to say e.g. 'a car' or 'a man' in Arabic, we just say 'car' or 'man'. So to say '**a big car**', we simply need to say '**car big**' (since we have already seen that the adjective comes after the noun).

However, when we add the word 'the' ('*al-*'), in Arabic it is added to both the noun and adjective. This means to say 'the big car', we first reverse the order ('car big'), and then we add 'the' in front of both words – '**the car the big**'. So the adjective even agrees with the article of the noun in Arabic.

The other important issue that this resolves is because the verb 'to be' is dropped in the present tense, which means that 'the car is big' already becomes '**the car is big**' in Arabic, which can create a little confusion when first starting out in the language.

But it becomes easier when we see some examples.

A big car *Sayyarah kabeerah* [sigh-yah-rah kah-beer-ah]
The big car *Al-sayyarah al-kabeerah* [al sigh-yah-rah al kah-beer-ah]
The car is big *Al-sayyarah kabeerah* [al sigh-yah-rah kah-beer-ah]
  (*Al-sayyarah ~~yakon~~ kabeerah*)
Big cars *Sayyarat kibar* [sigh-yah-rah'y ki-bar]

A good boy *Walad jayyid* [wah-lad jigh-id]
The good boy *Al-walad al-jayyid* [al wah-lad al jigh-id]
The boy is good *Al-walad ~~yakon~~ jayyid* [al wah-lad jigh-id]
Good boys *Awlad jayyidoon* [ow-lad jigh-id-oon]

Delicious food *Ta'am lazeez* [taah'm lah-zeez]
The delicious food *Al-ta'am al-lazeez* [al taah'm al lah-zeez]
The food is delicious *Al-ta'am lazeez* [al taah'm lah-zeez]

Note the following in the above examples:
1. 'a ___ ___ ' > noun adjective (m. or f.)
2. 'the ___ ___ ' > al-noun al-adjective (m. or f.)
3. 'the ___ is ___ ' > al-noun adjective (m. or f.)
4. '___ ___ s' > pl. noun pl. adjective

8b. Some Common Adjectives

Given in the format:
M: *masculine (plural)*   [pronunciation]
F: *feminine (plural)*   [pronunciation]

Good
M: *jayyid (-oon)*   [jigh-id (-oon)]
F: *jayyidah (-at)*   [jigh -id-ah (-ah't)]

Bad
M: *sayye'e (sayye'oon)*   [say'yih ('-oon)]
F: *sayye'ah (-at)*   [say'yah (-ah't)]

Big
M: *kabeer (kibar (pl.))*   [kah-beer (ki-bar)]
F: *kabeerah (-at)*   [kah-beer-ah (-ah't)]

Small
M: *sagheer (seghar)*   [sah-RR-eer]
F: *sagheerah (-at)*   [sah-RR-eer-ah]

Expensive
M: *ghaly* (pl. not really used)   [RR'air-lee]
F: ghalyah   [RR'air-lee'ah]

Cheap
M: *rakhees*   [rah-KHees]
F: *rakheesah*   [rah-KHee-sah]

Beautiful
M: *jameel* [jah-meel] (pl. jomal but rarely used)   [jah-meel (joh-mal)]
F: *jameelah (-at)*   [jah-meel-ah (-ah't)]
(**Beauty** – *jamal*)

Delicious
M: *lazeez*   [lah-zeez]
F: *lazeezah*   [lah-zee-zah]

33

8c. Comparatives / Superlatives (e.g. 'bigger' and 'biggest')

To use these is easy in Arabic. With these, there are no changes for gender or plural, and it is just a question of learning the words.

Good – better – the best
jayyid – ajwad – al-ajwad   [jigh-id / ah'j-wah'd]

Bad – worse – the worst
sayye'e – aswa'a – al-aswa'a   [say'yih / ah-swah]

Big – bigger – the biggest
kabeer – akbar – al-akbar   [kah-beer / ak-bar]

Small – smaller – the smallest
sagheer – asghar – al-asghar   [sah-RR-eer / ah-s'RR'ah'r]

Expensive – more expensive – the most expensive
ghaly – aghla – al-aghla   [RR-eh-lee / ah-RR-lah]

Cheap – cheaper – the cheapest
rakhees – arkhas – al-arkhas   [rah-KH-ee'ss / arr-KH-us]

9. Questions & Question Words

As was briefly noted in the Verbs (Part 1) chapter, forming questions in Arabic is very simple.

'hal'

All you have to do is add the word 'hal' before the sentence, and this makes it into a question. When you speak, you can use a questioning tone like in English. You can also just say the sentence without even using the word 'hal', as long as you use a questioning tone, and this will suffice in Arabic.

You see her *Anta taraha* [an-tah tah-rah-hah]
Do you see her? *Hal anta taraha?* [hal an-tah tah-rah-hah]

You are Egyptian *Anta Masry / Anti Masryyah*
[an-tah mass-ree / an-tee mass-reh-yah]

Are you Egyptian? *Hal anta Masry / Hal anti Masryyah*
[hal an-tah mass-ree / an-tee mass-reh-yah]

He is American *Howa Amreky*
[hoh-wah ah'm-reh-kee]

Is he American? *Hal howa Amreky*
[hal hoh-wah ah'm-reh-kee]

Question Words

Using question words in Arabic couldn't be simpler. Just like we saw with '*hal*' above, the relevant question word is simply added at the start of the sentence. In English, this would be the equivalent of something like this:

"He is here" => Question: "WHY he is here?"
"We are going" => Question: "WHERE we are going?"

So, we just need to learn the question words, and then add them before the sentence.

What? *Maza?* [**mah**-zah]

Where? *Ayna?* [ay-nah]

Who? *Man?* [mah'n]

When? *Mata?* [mah-tah]

Why? *Lemaza?* [leh-**mah**-zah]

How? *Kayfa?* [kay-fah]

How much/many? *Kam?* [kah'm]

Examples

What? *Maza?* [**mah**-zah]

What does that mean?
Maza ya'ani zalek? [mah-zah yah'ah-nee zah-lek]

What do you want?
Maza (anta) toreed? [mah-zah toh-reed]

What do you want to drink?
Maza (anta) toreed an tashrab? [mah-zah toh-reed an tah'sh-rah'b]

What are you doing?
Maza (anta) tafaal? [mah-zah tah-faah'l]

Where? *Ayna* [ay-nah]

Where is Tahrir Square?
Ayna Medan Al-Tahrir? [ay-nah meh-dan tah-H'rear]

Where are we going?
Ayna (nahnu) nazhab? [ay-nah **naz**-hah'b]

Who? *Man?* [mah'n]

Who is this? ("Who?")
Man? [mah'n]

Who is coming? ("Who will come?")
Man sa-ya'ate? [mah'n sah-yah'ah-teh]

When? *Mata?* [mah-tah]

When are we going?
Mata (nahnu) nazhab? [mah-tah **naz**-hah'b]

When do you want to go?
Mata (anta) toreed an tazhab? [mah-tah toh-reed an taz-hah'b]

When is the next train to Alexandria?
Mata al-ketar at-taly ela al-eskandaria?
[mah-tah al-keh-tahr at-tah-lee al-eh-skan-dah-ree'ah]

Why? *Lemaza?* [leh-**mah**-zah]

Why don't you like him / her?
Lemaza (anta) la-toheboh? (him) [leh-**mah**-zah lah-toh-heh-boh]
Lemaza (anta) la-toheboha? (her) [leh-**mah**-zah lah-toh-heh-boh-hah]

How? *Kayfa?* [kay-fah]

How do I eat this?
Kayfa (ana) akol haza? [kay-fah aah-kol **hah**-zah]

How do I get to Tahrir Square?
Kayfa (ana) azhab ela Medan Al-Tahrir?

How much / How many?   *Kam*   [kah'm]

How much is this?
There are 2 ways to say this:

Kam thaman haza?   [kah'm thah'mah'n **hah**-zah]
("How much is the price of this?")

Bikam haza?   [be-kah'm **hah**-zah]
("How much is this?")

What time is it? (lit. "How many hours?")
Kam as-sa'a?   [kah'm ass-sah'ah]

10. Numbers and Counting

10a. General

Learning Arabic numbers is straightforward. Just like in English, we need to learn numbers 1-19 individually, and then the tens (20, 30, 40 etc), hundreds and thousands.

0	*sifr*	[sif'r]
1	*wahid*	[**wah**-hid]
2	*ithnan*	[ith-**nah'n**]
3	*thalathah*	[thah-**lah**-thah]
4	*arba'ah*	[ar-bah'ah]
5	*khamsah*	[**KH'am**-sah]
6	*sittah*	[sit-ah]
7	*sab'ah*	[sab-aah]
8	*thamaniyah*	[thah-**mah**-ni-yah]
9	*tis'ah*	[tiss-ah]
10	*asherah*	[ah-sheh-rah]

For numbers 11-20, we use a form of the first 9 numbers plus a shortened form of 10.

11	*ahad ashar*	[ah-had ash-ar]
12	*ithna ashar*	[ith-nah ash-ar]
13	*thalathah ashar*	[thah-lah-thah ash-ar]
14	*arba'ata ashar*	[ar-bah'ah-tah ash-ar]
15	*khamsata ashar*	[KH'am-sah-tah ash-ar]
16	*sittata ashar*	[sitt-ah-tah ash-ar]
17	*sab'ata ashar*	[sab-ah-tah ash-ar]
18	*thamaniyata ashar*	[thah-mah-ni-yah-tah ash-ar]
19	*tis'ata ashar*	[tiss-ah-tah ash-ar]

Next, let's look at the tens, and then we can look at how to form other numbers

20	*ishrun*	[ish-roon]
30	*thalathun*	[thah-lah-thoon]
40	*arba'un*	[ar-bah-oon]
50	*khamsun*	[KH'am-soon]
60	*sittun*	[sitt-oon]
70	*sab'un*	[sab-oon]
80	*thamanun*	[thah-mah-noon]
90	*tis'un*	[tiss-oon]

And to construct the numbers using these, the format is actually the same as most Germanic languages in Europe, and will be easy if anyone is familiar with those languages. Anyway, it is not complicated, and simply involves saying the following:

21 = One and twenty
25 = Five and twenty
38 = Eight and thirty
And so on…

(**and** = '*wa*', pronounced [*wah*])

So using the above examples:
21 *wahid wa ishrun* [wah-hid wah ish-roon]
25 *khamsah wa ishrun* [KH'am-sah wah ish-roon]
38 *thamaniyah wa thalathun* [thah-mah-nee-yah wah thah-lah-thoon]

When saying the hundreds, note that the word for 200 is different, and for the rest, we just need the word for 'hundred / one hundred', and then it is similar to English, e.g. "Three hundred", "Four hundred" etc.

100 *mi'ah* [**mee**-yah]
200 *mitayn* [mit-ain]
300 *thalathah mi'ah* [thah-lah-tah mee-yah]
500 *khamsah mi'ah* [KH'am-sah mee-yah]
800 *thamaniyah mi'ah* [thah-mah-ni-yah mee-yah]

As with the hundreds, 2,000 stands out from the rest. Then for 3,000 and above, we use the plural of 'thousand'.

1,000 *alf* ("thousand") [alf]
2,000 *alfayn* ("two thousand") [alf-ain]
3,000 *thalathah aalaf* ("three thousands") [thah-lah-tah aah-laf]
5,000 *khamsah aalaf* ("five thousands") [KH;am-sah aah-laf]
8,000 *thamaniyah aalaf* ("eight thousands") [thah-mah-ni-yah aah-laf]

Then, to make more complex numbers, it is a case of stating the numbers as mentioned above, in order from largest to smallest.

Examples

3,495   "3 thousands, 4 hundred, 5 and 90"
thalathah aalaf arba'ah mi'ah khamsah wah tis'un
[thah-lah-thah aah-laf ar-bah'ah mee-yah KH'am-sah wah tiss-oon]

5, 231   "5 thousands, 2 hundred, 1 and 30"
khamsah aalaf mitayn wahid wah thalathun`
[KH'am-sah aah-laf mit-ayn wah-hid wah thah-lah-thoon]

9,999   "9 thousands, 9 hundred, 9 and 90"
tis'ah aalaf tis'ah mi'ah tis'ah wah tis'un
[tiss-ah aah-laf tiss-ah mee-yah tiss-ah wah tiss-oon]

8,025   "8 thousands, 5 and 20"
thamaniyah aalaf khamsah wah ishrun
[thah-mah-nee-yah aah-laf KH'am-sah wah ish-roon]

Finally, if you ever need even higher numbers, these two are easily recognisable…
Million   *milyon*   [mil-yon]
Billion   *bilyon*   [bil-yon]

Easy Practice
Work out these numbers in Arabic: 150, 725, 932, 1,234, 5,585.

10b. Stating how many

In Arabic, saying '3 or more' of something is just like English (i.e. state the number plus the plural noun, like '3 dogs' or 'some dogs'). But when talking about 1 or 2 of something, there are some differences from English (see points A and B below, and then a more in-depth breakdown and examples will be given afterwards).

A. How to specify 'one + noun' (e.g. '1 dog')

To state a noun in the singular, you can just state the noun alone (to mean 'a/an' + noun). But if you want to specify that it is one of something, then you obviously need to add the Number 1. However, Number 1 is used differently to the other numbers in Arabic, and is not treated like a number at all. In fact, 'one' becomes an adjective when used with a noun. This means that it also follows the rules we have seen for adjectives – namely that 'one' follows the noun, and also agrees with the noun's gender.

So, to say 'one + noun', we need to see if the noun is masculine or feminine and then use the relevant word ending for it. This will become clear if we look at some examples.

Masculine (no change in the ending):
1 man   *rajol wahid*   [rah-jol wah-hid]
1 shop   *mahal wahid*   [mah-hal wah-hid]

Feminine (ends in '-ah'):
1 girl   *bent wahedah*   [bent wah-heh-dah]
1 car   *sayyarah wahedah*   [sigh-yah-rah wah-heh-dah]

Remember that to say e.g. 'a man' or 'a woman', it is just a case of stating the noun by itself, so you can avoid using the number one unless you really want to specify it.

B. How to specify 'two + noun' (e.g. '2 dogs')

In Arabic, there is a special way to say '2 of something'. This means that where, in English, we have singular (dog) and plural (dogs), in Arabic, there are three forms: singular (dog), dual (2 dogs) and plural (3 or more dogs).

So now let's break it all down and look at some examples of each situation, Single, Dual & Plural.

Single

This is, very simply, just like English: 'a', 'the' or 'one' of something.
For example, '**a car**' – *sayyarah*, '**the car**' – *al-sayyarah*, '**one car**' – *sayyarah wahedah* (remember 'one' comes after the noun in Arabic).

Dual

This is where Arabic has an extra form, but it is easy to use. To say 2 of something, we just need to add '-*an*' ('-an' for correct Arabic, or '-*ayn*' as it is usually pronounced) onto the end of the noun. For feminine nouns ending in '-*ah*', the ending becomes '-*tan*'.

Examples:

Man *rajol* [rah-jol]
2 men *rajolan* [rah-jol-an]

Girl *bent* [bent]
2 girls *bentan* [ben-tan]

Car *sayyarah* [sigh-yah-rah]
2 cars *sayyaratan* [sigh-yah-rah-tan]

Student *taleb (m.) / talebah (f.)* [tah-leb / tah-leb-ah]
2 students *taleban (m.) / talebatan (f.)* [tah-leb-an / tah-leb-ah-tan]

Plural

So in Arabic, the plural only begins with 3 or more of something. This can take a little getting used to, but once it has sunk in, it becomes very straightforward. So the word '*sayyarat*', which means 'cars', indicates at least 3 cars.

Examples

1 car *sayyarah wahedah* [sigh-yah-rah wah-hed-ah]
2 cars *sayyaratan* [sigh-yah-rah-tah'n]
3 cars *thalathah sayyarat* [thah-lah-thah sigh-yah-rah't]

The drink *al-mashroob* [al-mash-roob]
2 drinks *mashrooban* [mash-roo-bah'n]
5 drinks *khamsat mashroobat* [KH'am-sat mash-roo-bah't]

A lady *sayyidah* [sigh-yid-ah]
2 ladies *sayyidatan* [sigh-yid-ah-tah'n]
Several ladies (3 or more) *sayyidat* [sigh-yid-ah't]

10c. Telling the time

Telling the time in Arabic is fairly straightforward. We just need to learn the words for 'hour', 'past', 'to', 'quarter' and 'half'. Also, the word for 'hour' is feminine, and the numbers have feminine forms, which will be given below – these are used to tell the time.

Asking: **What time is it?**   *Kam as-sa'a?*   [kah'm ass-sah'ah]
(Literally means: "How many the hour?" – *'sa'a'* = 'hour').

The simplest format to say the time is as follows:

1. State the hour (the number in the feminine form)
1   *al-wahedah*   [al-**wah**-hed-ah]
2   *al-thaniyah*   [al-**thah**-ni-yah]
3   *al-thaleethah*   [al-thaah-**lee**-thah]
4   *ar-rabe'eeah*   [ah'RR-ah-**beh**'ah]
5   *al-khameesah*   [al-KH'am-**ee**-sah]
6   *as-sadeesah*   [ass-sah-**dee**-sah]
7   *as-sabee'ah*   [ass-sah-**beh**'ah]
8   *al-thameenah*   [al-thah-**mee**-nah]
9   *at-tase'eah*   [at-tah-**seh**'ah]
10   *al-asherah*   [al-**aah**-sheh-rah]
11   *al-hadeeta asherah*   [al-hah-dee-eh't-ah aah-sheh-rah]
12   *al-thaniyata asherah*   [al-thah-nee-yah-tah aah-sheh-rah]

2. If it is not exactly on the hour, state 'past' or 'to' followed by the number of minutes.
Past ('and')   *wa*   [wah]
To ('minus')   *ella*   [el-lah]
So,
Five past...   *...wa khamsah*   [wah KH'am-sah]
Five to...   *...ella khamsah*   [el-lah KH'am-sah]
Ten past...   *...wa asherah*   [wah ah-sheh-rah]
Ten to...   *...ella asherah*   [el-lah ah-sheh-rah]

3. Alternatively to no. 2 above, if it is 'half past' or 'quarter past / to', then it is the same, but using the word for 'half' or 'quarter' instead of the minutes. Interestingly, Arabic also uses the word for 'third' (20 minutes), so you can also say 'a third past' and 'a third to'.

Half   *nesf*   [nes-fuh]
Quarter   *rob'a*   [roh-bah]
Third   *tholth*   [thool'th]
So,
Half past…   *…wa nesf*   [wah nes-fuh]
Quarter past…   *…wa rob'a*   [wah roh-bah]
Quarter to…   *…ella rob'a*   [el-lah roh-bah]
20 (a third) past   *…wa tholth*   [wah thool'th]
20 (a third) to   *…ella tholth*   [el-lah thool'th]

4. Then, if you wish, you can add the words for a.m. & p.m.
A.M.   *Sabahan*   [sah-bah-han]
P.M.   *Masa'an*   [mah-sah-an]

5. There is a special case for 12:00, either a.m. or p.m. In Arabic, these times are stated as "12 midnight" and "12 noon".
12 midnight   *12 laylan*   [leh-lan]
12 noon   *12 zohran*   [zoh-hran]

And that's it. Let's see a quick summary and then some examples.

Summary
- Feminine Number Form (e.g. *al-wahedah*)
- *wa* (past/and) / *ella* (to/minus)
- Minutes / *nesf* / *rob'a* / *tholth*
- *Sabahan* / *Masa'an*

Examples

1:00
Al-wahedah
[al wah-heh-dah]

1:15 ('1:00 and quarter')
Al-wahedah wa nesf wa khamsah
[al wah-heh-dah wah nes-fuh wah KH'am-sah]

1:25 ('1:00 and 5-and-20')
Al-wahedah wa khamsah wa ishrun
[al wah-heh-dah wah KH'am-sah wah ish-roon]

7:50 a.m. ('8:00 minus 10')
As-sabee'ah ella asherah sabahan
[ass-sah-beh'ah] al-lah ah-sheh-rah sah-bah-han]

4:30 p.m. ('4:00 and half')
Ar-rabe'eeah wa nesf masa'an
[aRR-ah-beh'ah wah nes-fuh mah-sah-an]

9:40p.m. ('10:00 minus 20')
Al-asherah ella tholth masa'an
[al ah-sheh-rah el-lah thool'th mah-sah-an]

Also note that there can be multiple ways of saying the same time in Arabic, using various combinations of the above. You can see these in the Advanced Language section on page 64.

Easy Practice
Work out these times as above:
6:30a.m., 9:45a.m., 3:10p.m., 5:30 p.m., 11:20 p.m.

11. Other Useful Words & Phrases

Answering Questions

Yes *Na'am* [naah'm]
No *La* [laah]
Ok *mowafek* [m'ow-ah-fek] (lit. "I agree")

I don't know *(Ana) la a'areef / a'arif* [(ah-nah) lah aah-rif]
I don't understand *(Ana) lam afham* [(ah-nah) lah af-hah'm]
(lit. "I didn't understand")

Sorry *A'asif / Ozran* [aah-sif / oh'z-ran]
No problem *la moshkelah* [lah moosh-keh-lah]

Modifying

A lot / much / many *katheer* [kah-th'ear]
A little / a few *kaleel* [kah-leel]

Too / very *jeddan* (f. *jeddanah*)
e.g. *katheer(-ah) jeddan(-ah)* = **too much / very much**
e.g. *kabeer(-ah) jeddan(-ah)* = **too big / very big**

Distinguishing

This *haza* (m) / *hazehe* (f) [hah-zee-hee]
That *zalek* [**zaah**-lik] (m) / *telk* [teh'lk] (f)
These/Those (m./f.) *ha'ola* [hah-oo'lah]

Here *hona* [hoh-nah]
There *honak* [hoh-nak]

Time

Today *al-yawm* [al-ee'yow'm]
Tomorrow *ghadan* [**RR'ah**-dan]
Yesterday *ams* [am'ss]
The day after tomorrow *ba'ad al-ghadd* [bah-ah'd al-RR'ud]
The day before yesterday *awwala ams* [ow'ah'lah am'ss]

Now *al-aan* [al-ahh'n]

Place

At / in   *fi*   [fee]
*(*Tom is at the hotel – *Tom fi al-fondok)*
*(*I am in Amman – *Ana fi Amman)*

On   *ala*   [ah-lah]
*(*The food is on the table – *Al-ta'am ala al-tawelah)*

To   *ela*   [eh-lah]
*(*We go to school – *Nahnu nazhab ela al-madrasa)*

From   *men*   [men]
*(*I am from Egypt - *Ana men Misr)*

PHRASES & CONVERSATION

12. Basic Conversation Questions and How to Answer Them

If you are in the Middle East for any length of time, it will really enhance your trip to be able to make some conversation with local people, no matter how basic. You will find people very appreciative of your efforts to speak their language, and it is a great opportunity to make some new friends.

1. **Where are you from?**   *Men ayna anta (anti)?*

2. **What's your name?**   *Ma esmak (esmek)?*

3. **How old are you?**   *Kam omrak (omrek)?*

4. **Are you married?**   *Hal anta (anti) motazawwej(-a)?*

5. **Do you have children?**   *Hal ladayka (ladayki) atfal?*

6. **What do you do?**   *Maza ta'amal (ta'amaleen)?*

Being able to ask and answer these few questions will help you survive in many basic conversations with local people.

1. Where are you from?   ("From where you?")
Men ayna anta (anti)?   [men ay-nah an-tah (an-tee)]

As we have seen earlier in the book, to say "I am English / American" etc in Arabic, we don't need the verb 'to be' so we simply say, "I English" or "I American" and so on. The only thing to ensure is that we use the correct gender for ourselves, for example, an English man will say "Ana Englezy", while an English woman should say "Ana Englezyya".

I am + nationality

Ana + (choose from the following list)

A list of nationalities is given below (If your country is not on here, just ask in your hotel how to say it):

English   *Englezy (m.), Englezyyah (f.)*   [en-gleh-zee (en-gleh-zee-yah)]

Scottish   *Scotlandy, Scotlandyyah*   [scot-lan-dee (-yah)]

Irish   *Irelandy, Irelandyyah*   [ear-lan-dee (-yah)]

American   *Amreeky, Amreekyyah*   [am-ree-kee (-yah)]

Canadian   *Canady, Canadyyah*   [kah-nah-dee (-yah)]

Australian   *Australy, Australyyah*   [oh-strah-lee (-yah)]

New Zealander   *New-Zealandy, New-Zealandyyah*
[new zee-lan-dee (-yah)]

French   *Faransy, Faransyyah*   [fah-ran-see (-yah)]

German   *Almany, Almanyyah*   [al-mah-nee (-yah)]

Italian   *Italy, Italyyah*   [ee-tah-lee (-yah)]

Spanish   *Espany, Espanyyah*   [ess-pah-nee (-yah)]

Russian   *Roosy, Roosyyah*   [roo-see (-yah)]

Do you speak … (language)?
Hal tatahaddath…?   [hal tah-tah-hah-dath]

English   *Al-Engleezyya*   [al-en-gleh-zee-yah]
Arabic   *Al- Arabiyyah*   [al-ah-rah-bay-ah]
French   *Al-Faransyya*   [al-fah-ran-say-ah]
German   *Al-Almanyya*   [al-al-mah-nee-yah]
Italian   *Al-Italyya*   [al-ee-tah-lee-yah]
Spanish   *Al-Espanyya*   [al-esp-ah-nee-yah]
Russian   *Al-Roosyya*   [al-roo-see-yah]

I speak (a little)
Atahaddath (kaleelan)   [at-ah-hah-dath (kah-leel-an)]

No, I can't speak it
La, la astate'e tahadotho-ha   [la, la ah-stah-teh'eh tah-hah-doh-thah-hah]

2.What's your name?
Ma esmak / esmek? (m / f)   [mah ess-mak / ess-mek]

My name's Peter
Esmy Peter   [ess-mee…]

What about you?
Maza anta / anti?   [mah-zah an-tah / an-tee]

3. How old are you?
Kam omrok (omrek)? (m / f)   [kah'm oh'm-rok / oh'm-rek]

I am (20)
Omry (ishrun)   [oh'm-ree…]

What about you?
Maza anta / anti?   [mah-zah an-tah / an-tee]

See Numbers Chapter on page 39 for numbers to say your age.

4.Are you married?
Hal anta motazawwej (m.) / anti motazawweja (f.)?
[hal an-tah moh-tah-zow-wedge (-weh-jah)]

 Yes I am
Na'am, ana motazawwej (m.) / motazawweja (f.)
[naah'm, ah-nah moh-tah-zah-wedge (-weh-jah)]

No I'm not
La, ana lasto motazawej (m.) / motazaweja (f.)
[laah, ah-nah lass-too moh-tah-zah-wedge (-weh-jah)]

This is my husband   *Haza zawjy*   [**hah-**zah zow-jee]

This is my wife   *Hazehe zawjaty*   [hah-zee-hee zow-jah-tee]

I have a boyfriend
Endy sadeek   [en-dee sah-deek]

I have a girlfriend
Endy sadeeka   [en-dee sah-dee-kah]

5. Do you have children?
Hal endaka (endaki) atfal? (m / f)
[hal end-ah-kah (en-dah-kee) at-faahl]

I have a (or **1**) **child**
Endy tefl   [en-dee tef'l]

I have 2 children
Endy teflan   [en-dee tef-lah'n]

1 son and 1 daughter   ("Boy and girl")
Walad wa bent   [wah-lad wah bent]

I don't have children
Laysa endy atfal   lay-sah en-dee at-faah'l]

6. What do you do?
Ma amalok?   [mah ah-mah-lok]

This is where you will have to find out or look up your own occupation – Ask at your hotel if they can help you.

I am (a teacher)
Ana mudarris (m.), Ana mudarrisah (f.)
[ah-nah moo-dah-rr'is (-sah)]

I am (a student)
Ana taleb (m.), Ana talebah...(f.)
[ah-nah tah-leb (-ah)]

13. Situational Arabic

In a Taxi

Go to...
Ezhab ela... [ez-hah'b eh-lah]

Turn right *Ed-khol yamenan* [ed-KH'ol yah-meh-nan]
Turn left *Ed-khol yasaran* [ed-KH'ol yah-sah-ran]
Go straight *Emshi mostakeman* [ed-KH'ol yah-meh-nah'n]

Stop here *Tawakkaf hona* [tow-ak-af hoh-nah]

Here *Hona* [hoh-nah]
There *Honak* [hoh-nak]

Turn around
or **Do a u-turn** *A'amel u-turn* [ah'ah-mel 'u-turn']

(At the) traffic light *(Eind) esharet al-moror*
[*(eye'nd) eh-shah-ret al-moh-roar*]

Up ahead *Amamak* [ah-mah-mak]

Go faster *Asre'e* [ass-reh'eh]
Slow down *Khafef as-sora'a* [KH'ah-fef ass-soh-raah]

Asking for Directions:

Where is Tahrir Square? *Ayna Medan Al-Tahrir?*

How do I get to Tahrir Square? *Kayfa azhab ela Medan Al-Tahrir?*

Example of a Simple Journey:

Hello. Go to Tahrir Square *Assalamu alaykum, ezhab ela Medan Al-Tahrir*

Go on (Talaat Harb) *Ezhab fi (Talaat Harb)*

At the lights, turn right, then turn left.
Eind al-eshara, edkhol yamenan thoma edkhol yasaran.

Ok stop here. Thank you. *Tawakkaf hona. Shukran.*

In a Bar or Coffee Shop

Ordering

I want (no.) bottles of (water)
Oreed (no.) zogagat men (al-ma'a)
[oh-reed … zoh-gah-gat men al-maah]

Bring (no.) glasses of (tea)
Ahder (no.) akwab men (al-shay)
[aH-deer … ak-wab men al-shay]

Numbers for ordering
1. *wahid*   [**wah**-hid]
2. *ithnan*   [ith-**nah'n**]
3. *thalathah*   [thah-**lah**-thah]
4. *arba'ah*   [ar-bah'ah]
5. *khamsah*   [**KH'am**-sah]
6. *sittah*   [**sit**-ah]
7. *sab'ah*   [**sab**-ah]
8. *thamaniyah*   [thah-**mah**-nee-yah]
9. *tis'ah*   [**tis**-ah]
10. *asherah*   [**ah**-sheh-rah]

Drinks

Non-alcoholic:

Water   *Meyah*   [mey-ah]
Mineral water   *meyah ma'adaneyah*   [mey-ah maah-dah-ney-ah]
Coffee   *kahwa*   [kah-wah]
Tea   *shay*   [shay]
Orange juice   *aseer bortokal*   [ah-seer bor-toh-kah'l]
Sugarcane (juice)   *ah-sab*   [ah-sah'b]

Branded drinks tend to be the same, e.g. *Coca-cola, Sprite* etc

Alcoholic:

Beer   *beerah*   [beer-ah]
White wine   *nabeez abyad*   [nah-beez ah-bee'ad]
Red wine   *nabeez ahmar*   [nah-beez ah-h'mar]

Stronger drinks tend to be the same, e.g. *whisky*, *vodka* etc.

I don't want ice   *La oreed thalj*   [lah oh-reed thahl'j]

Do you have cold ones?
Hal ladayka bared men haza?   [hal lah-day-kah bah-red men **hah**-zah]

In a Restaurant

Getting a Table
People   *ashkhas*   [ash-KH-ah'ss]
(**How many people?**
Kam adad al-ashkhas?   [kah'm ah-dad al-ash-KH-ah'ss])
(**3 / 4 people**
Thalathah / Arba'ah ashkhas   [thah-lah-thah / ar-baah ash-KH-ah'ss])

Food
Beef   *Lahm bakary*   [lah'm bah-kah-ry]
Chicken   *Dajaj*   [dah-jah'j]
Lamb   *Lahm ghanam*   [lah'm RR'ah-nah'm]
Pork   *Lahm khanzeer*   [lah'm KH'an-zeer]
Fish   *Samak*   [sah-mak]
Vegetables   *Khodrawat*   [KH'oh-drah-wat]
Vegetarian dishes   *Atbak nabatyyah*   [at-bak nah-bah-tay-yah]
 (**I'm a vegetarian**   *Ana nabaty*   [ah-nah nah-bah-tee])
Rice   *Aroz*   [ah-roz]

Ordering
We want {1 / 2 / 3…}   *Noreed*   [noh-reed]
Bring   {1 / 2 / 3…}   *Ahder lana*   [ah-h'dar lah-nah]

Glass   *Koob*   [koob]
Bottle   *Zogagah*   [zoh-gah-gah]
Plate / Dish (incl. for rice)   *Tabak (pl. Atbak)*   [tah-bak / at-bak]
Bowl (e.g. for soup)   *Boola*   [boo-lah]

Useful Language

Waiter   *Garson* or "*nadel*"   [gar-sonn / nah-del]
Check / Bill   *Al-check/Al-fatoorah*   [al-check / al-fah-too-rah]
 (i.e. to request the check / bill: *"Garson! Al-check / Al-fatoorah!"*)

Spicy   *har*   [harr]
 (Is this one spicy? – *Hal haza har?*)
 (I don't want it spicy – *La oreedo har*)

Menu   *Menu*   ['menu']
(Do you have an **English menu**? – *Hal ladayk **menu bel engleezyah**?*)

Example of a simple visit:

"Hello, how many people?"
"Marhaban, kam adad al-ashkhas?"

4 people.
Arba'ah ashkhas

...

Waiter!
Garson!

I want a kebab and kofta
Oreed kabab wa kofta

Bring 4 dishes of rice
Ahder lana arba'ah atbak men al aroz

Do you have tea? Ok, bring 4 glasses of tea.
Hal ladayka shay? Hasanan, Ahder lana arba'ah akwab men al-shay.

Thank you.
Shukran lak.

...

Waiter! Check, please!
Garson, al-fatoorah men fadlak!

Thank you.
Shukran lak.

In a Shop

Price & Bargaining

How much is this?
Bikam haza?   [be-**kah'm hah**-zah]
Kam thaman haza?   [kah'm thah'mah'n **hah**-zah]
 ('*thaman*' = 'price')

100 Pounds
Mi'at Gneeh   [mee'at gn'eh]

It's too expensive
Ghali jeddan   [RR'ah-lee jed-an]

I'll give you 50 Pounds
Sa-o'teek khamseen Gneeh   [sah-oh-teek KH'am-seen gn'eh]

Size and Colour

Do you have bigger?
Hal ladayka akbar?   [hal lah-day-kah ak-bar]

Do you have smaller?
Hal ladayka asghar?   [hal lah-day-kah ass-RR'ar]

Do you have another colour?
Hal ladayka lawn aakhar?   [hal lah-day-kah l'ow'n ah'ah-KH-ar]

Making Your Purchase

I want this
Oreedo haza   [oh-reh-doh **hah**-zah]

I don't want that
La oreedo haza   [lah oh-reh-doh **hah**-zah]

I want the receipt
Oreedo al-fatoora   [oh-reh-doh al-fah-toor-ah]

Money / Currency

In Arabic, the terms **Dollar** and **Rial** are the same as English, and the word for **Pounds** is '*Gneeh*'

Dollar – dollar
Rial – rial
Pound (Sterling) – Gneeh (Sterling) [g'neh]

This is 50 Pounds
Hazehe khamseen Gneeh   [hah-zee-hee Ham-seen gn'eh]

120 Dollars
Mi'ah wa ishreen Dollar   [mee-yah wah ish-reen gn'eh]

MORE ADVANCED
LANGUAGE

14. Extra Vocab

Short Words, Conjunctions etc

Note that some of these are 'general equivalents' since, as when you learn other languages, some prepositions and conjunctions are used slightly differently in different languages – consider how varied their use is in English too: 'on the table', 'on Monday', 'on time', 'by 8:00', 'by the station', 'by myself' and so on. To really get to grips with these, you need to spend time learning them in detail. For basic understanding, however, using these as general equivalents will get you by for the most part.

And   *wa*   [wah]
But   *laken*   [laah-ken]
So   *lezalek*   [leh-zah-lek]
Because   *besabab*   [beh-**sah**-bab]
Or   *aw*   [ow]
If   *law*   [l'ow]
For   *le*   [leh]

Prepositions
In / at   *fi*   [fee]
Out   *khareg*   [KH'ah-reg]
On   *a'ala*   [ah'ah-lah]
To   *ela*   [eh-lah]
From   *men*   [men]
With   *ma'a*   [maah]
Before   *kabl*   [kah'bl]
After   *ba'ad*   [bah-ah'd]
Up/over   *fawk*   [fowk]
Down/under   *taht*   [ta'H't]

15. Verbs (Part 2): Verb Grades, Simple Past, Past Continuous & Giving Orders

15a. General

On top of the earlier section on verbs, there is some more complicated grammar around Arabic verbs than mentioned previously, which will be shown in this chapter.

Key Things to Note

- Arabic verbs have 3 main "Verb grades" (past tense, present tense, & giving orders), which are usually shown in a table, as you will see. These "verb grades" are then used to form the various verb tenses. "Verb grades" are the first thing covered in this chapter below.

- The 4 tenses that will enable you to get by in Arabic are the Present, the Future, the Simple Past and the Past Continuous. We have already covered the Present and Future Tenses. In this chapter, the two past tenses will be added.

- Then, the 'order grade' will be introduced. This is the 'imperative' of the verb, or in other words, how to give orders (e.g. 'Go!').

15b. Verb Grades

We have already learned the present and future tenses of the verbs, and before we see the verb forms for the other tenses, let us see how verbs are learned in Arabic, since it is different to English.

For each verb, there are three main forms, or **3 verb grades**. These grades are **Past – Present – Order**, i.e. the past tense, the present tense and the form of the verb used to give an order (the 'imperative' in English). The various tenses and verb forms in Arabic are formed from these 3 verb grades.

So verbs are learned in Arabic in these 3 grades. The **past tense** form, the **present tense** form and the **order** form, as we can see in the following table.

Verb - Past - Present - Order

Arrive - *Wasal* - *Yasel* - *Sel*
Come - *Ata* - *Ya'ate* - *E'tee (Taal)*
Cook - *Tabakh* - *Yatbokh* - *Etbokh*
Do - *Faal* - *Yafaal* - *Efaal*
Drink - *Sharab* - *Yashrab* - *Eshrab*
Eat - *Akal* - *Ya'akol* - *Kol*
Get - *Ahdar* - *Yohder* - *Ahder*
Give - *A'ata* - *Yoote* - *A'ate*
Go - *Zahab* - *Yazhab* - *Ezhab*
Leave - *Tarak* - *Yatrok* - *Etrok*
Like - *Ahabb* - *Yohebb* - *Ahebb*
Look - *Nazar* - *Yanzor* - *Onzor*
Love - *Ahabb* - *Yohebb* - *Ahebb*
Play - *Laaeb* - *Yalaab* - *Elaab*
See - *Raa* - *Yara* - *N/A*
Speak - *Takallam* - *Yatakallam* - *Takallam*
Want - *Arad* - *Yoreed* - *Red*
Watch - *Shahad* - *Yoshahed* - *Shahed*

As we move onto the tenses, note that each tense begins from the relevant verb grade in the table above. What you can now see is that the present tense verbs we looked at earlier, which all began with '*Y-*' are shown here in the **Present** column above. E.g. we used '*Yazhab*' (to go), and now we can see it as 'Zahab – **Yazhab** – Ezhab' (in order: Past – Present – Order).

15c. Past Tenses

For Basic Arabic, we can get by if we learn two past tenses, the Simple Past ('I went', 'we played' etc), and the Past Continuous ('I was going', 'we were playing' etc). You could even manage with just the Simple Past, but the Past Continuous is included so that you have the luxury of using both (it is up to you though, if you choose to learn just the simple past).

Simple Past Tense

The Simple Past in Arabic is formed by taking the 'past' verb grade and making the relevant changes for each person (e.g. 'To Go': *Zahab – Yazhab – Ezhab.* With this verb, therefore, *Zahab* is the Past Tense).

To Go (Simple Past) – *Zahab*

I went   *Ana Zahabt*   Plus '-*t*'
We went   *Nahnu Zahabna*   Plus '-*na*'

You (m.) went   *Anta Zahabt*   Plus '-*t*'
You (f.) went   *Anti Zahabtee*   Plus '-*tee*'
You (pl.) went   *Antum Zahabtum*   Plus '-*tum*'

He went   *Howa Zahab*   No change
She went   *Heya Zahabat*   Plus '-*at*'
They went   *Hum Zahaboo*   Plus '-*oo*'

Examples

I went to school
Ana zahabt ela al-madrasa   [ah-nah zah-hab't eh-lah al-mah-drah-sah]

My friend saw the Pyramids
Sadeeky ra'a al-Ahramat   [sah-dee-kee rah'ah al-ah-rah-mat]

Negative for Simple Past (didn't do)

The Arabic word which forms the negative in the past is '*Lam*'. We can think of this as meaning '**didn't**', and it comes right before the verb, exactly like in English.

Just the same as in English, '**didn't**' is followed by the present tense. For example, we don't say, "I didn't went" in English, we say "I didn't go". The difference is that the verb is still conjugated in Arabic, so it goes more like this: "I didn't play", "He / She didn't plays", "They didn't play".

Didn't = *Lam* + Present Tense

So changing the examples above into the negative is very simple:

I went to school   *Ana zahabt ela al-madrasa*
[ah-nah zah-hab't eh-lah al-mah-drah-sah]

I didn't go to school   *Ana lam azhab ela al-madrasa*
[ah-nah lam az-hab eh-lah al-mah-drah-sah]

My friend saw the Pyramids   *Sadeeky ra'a al-Ahramat*
[sah-dee-kee rah'ah al ah-rah-mat]

My friend didn't see the Pyramids   *Sadeeky lam yara al-Ahramat*
[sah-dee-kee lam yah-rah al ah-rah-mat]

Past Continuous

This tense is the direct equivalent of the English, "I was –ing"). The Arabic construction uses the simple past of 'to be' like in English, but the verb that follows is conjugated, just as it was in the present tense. (i.e. in Arabic, it goes something like this: "I was do", "We were do", "He was does" etc). This is easy once you have learned the few verb forms for the present tense though.

The format below shows how to form the past continuous using the past of 'to be' with the verb 'to go', i.e. 'I was going' etc.

Pronoun – Past of 'to be' – 'going' (present)

I   *Ana – Kuntoo* [kuh'n-too] *– Azhab*
We   *Nahnu – Kunna* [kuh'n-nah] *– Nazhab*

You (m.)   *Anta – Kunta* [kuh'n-tah] *– Tazhab*
You (f.)   *Anti – Kunti* [kuh'n-tee] *– Tazhabeen*
You (pl.)   *Antum – Kuntum* [kuh'n-tuh'm] *– Tazhaboon*

He   *Howa – Kana* [kah-nah] *– Yazhab*
She   *Heya – Kanat* [kah-nah't] *– Tazhab*
They   *Hum – Kanoo* [kah-noo] *– Yazhaboon*

As you can see, the verb 'going' changes exactly as we have already learned, so it is just a case now of learning the verb 'to be' in the past, and then putting them together.

Below is another example, using the verb 'to play', in the past continuous.

I was playing   *Ana Kunto Alaab*
We were playing   *Nahnu Kunna Nalaab*

You (m.) were playing   *Anta Kunta Talaab*
You (f.) were playing   *Anti Kunti Talabeen*
You (pl.) were playing   *Antum Kuntum Talaboon*

He was playing   *Howa Kana Yalaab*
She was playing   *Heya Kanat Talaab*
They were playing   *Hum Kanoo Yalaboon*

Negative for Past Continuous (wasn't / weren't doing)

As with the past simple, the word for the negative in the past is '*Lam*' (= **didn't**), and is followed here by the **present tense** of 'to be' and then the **present tense** of the main verb.

So the form might seem strange to us, but the English equivalent would be this (and note that each verb, 'to be' as well as the main verb are changed just as in the regular present tense):
I didn't am play
He didn't is plays
They didn't are play

Examples

I wasn't playing   *Ana Lam Akon Alaab*
[ah-nah lam ah-kohn ah-laah'b]

He wasn't going   *Howa Lam Yakon Yazhab*
[hoh-wah lam yah-kohn yaz-hah'b]

They weren't watching (*Adv. Lang. 4 on page 77)
Hum Lam Yakonoon Yoshahedoon
[huh'm lam yah-koo-noon yoh-shah-heh-doon]

15d. Giving Orders

This is the easiest of the verb grades to learn since there are just 3 forms to learn (i.e. the 3 forms of You – You (male), You (female) and You (plural) – since these are all the possibilities that we can give orders to.

Let's look at the verb '**to go**' (*Zahab* – *Yazhab* – *__Ezhab__*), where the order grade it the third word '*Ezhab*'.

To use the order form of the verb is easy, and the verb changes as follows:

You (m.)   *Ezhab*   No change

You (f.)   *Ezhabi*   Adds '-*i*'
(unless already ends in '-*i*'– then no change)

You (m/f. pl)   *Ezhaboo*   Adds '-*oo*'
(although there is officially a further form for f. pl., this is not normally used)

Example
Go to school! (to one male)
Ezhab ela al-madrasa   [ez-hah'b eh-lah al mah-drah-sah]

15e. VERBS 2 SUMMARY

Verb Grades:
There are 3 'verb grades' in Arabic
Learned as "**Past – Present – Order**"
Each grade is conjugated
Each grade is used in different instances
Past: Simple past
Present: Present Tense, Future, Past Continuous, Negatives
Order: Used as an order

Simple Past Tense:
(Did, Went etc)
Uses Past Tense Verb Grade (the 1st one of the 3)
Ana: Plus '-t'
Nahnu: Plus -na'
Anta: Plus '-t'
Anti: Plus '-tee'
Antum: Plus '-tum'
Howa: No change
Heya: Plus '-at'
Hum: Plus '-oo'

Negative Simple Past:
(Didn't do / go etc)
'*Lam*' + Present Tense

Past Continuous Tense:
(Was / Were doing / going etc)
Simple Past of 'to be' + Present Tense of 'main verb'

Negative Past Continuous:
(Wasn't / Weren't doing / going etc)
'*Lam*' + Present 'to be' + Present 'main verb'

Ordering:
(Do this!)
Uses Order Verb Grade (the 3rd of the 3)
Anta: No change
Anti: Plus '-i'
Antum: Plus '-oo'

16. The Verb 'To Be' (Part 2)

Past Tense of 'To Be'

The past tense of 'to be' is the equivalent of 'was' / 'were' in English. See below for how to say this in Arabic.

'To be' – *Kan*

I was   *Ana Kunto*   [kuh'n-too]
We were   *Nahnu Kunna*   [kuh'n-nah]

You (m.) were   *Anta Kunta*   [kuh'n-tah]
You (f.) were   *Anti Kunti*   [kuh'n-tee]
You (pl.) were   *Antum Kuntum*   [kuh'n-tuh'm]

He was   *Howa Kana*   [kah-nah]
She was   *Heya Kanat*   [kah-nat]
They were   *Hum Kanoo*   [kah-noo]

Negative Past Tense of 'To Be'

I wasn't   *Ana Lam Akon*   [lam ah-kohn]
We weren't   *Nahnu Lam Nakon*   [lam nah-kohn]

You (m.) weren't   *Anta Lam Takon*   [lam tah-kohn]
You (f.) were   *Anti Lam Takoony*   [lam tah-koo-nee]
You (pl.) weren't   *Antum Lam Takoonoo*   [lam tah-koo-noo]

He wasn't   *Howa Lam Yakon*   [lam yah-kohn]
She wasn't   *Heya Lam Takon*   [lam tah-kohn]
They weren't   *Hum Lam Yakoonoo*   [lam yah-koo-noo]

Future Tense of 'To Be'

I will be   *Ana Sa-Akon*   [sah ah-kohn]
We will be   *Nahnu Sa-Nakon*   [sah nah-kohn]

You (m.) will be   *Anta Sa-Takon*   [sah tah-kohn]
You (f.) will be   *Anti Sa-Takoony*   [sah tah-koo-nee]
You (pl.) will be   *Antum Sa-Takoonoon*   [sah tah-koo-noon]

He will be   *Howa Sa-Yakon*   [sah yah-kohn]
She will be   *Heya Sa-Takon*   [sah tah-kohn]
They will be   *Hum Sa-Yakoonoon*   [sah yah-koo-noon]

Negative Future Tense of 'To Be'

I won't be   *Ana Lan Akon*   [lan ah-kohn]
We won't be   *Nahnu Lan Nakon*   [lan nah-kohn]

You (m.) won't be   *Anta Lan Takon*   [lan tah-kohn]
You (f.) won't be   *Anti Lan Takoony*   [lan tah-koo-nee]
You (pl.) won't be   *Antum Lan Takoonoo*   [lan tah-koo-noo]

He won't be   *Howa Lan Yakon*   [lan yah-kohn]
She won't be   *Heya Lan Takon*   [lan tah-kohn]
They won't be   *Hum Lan Yakoonoo*   [lan yah-koo-noo]

17. More Advanced Language Points

These language points are included just for those who wish to speak as properly as possible. However, we have separated it because they are unnecessary for communicating and being understood. Indeed, as mentioned in the introduction, many native Arabic speakers do not know or use a lot of the language's more advanced grammar, and many native speakers make mistakes with some of the same rules that follow here.

17a. The Definite Article – 'Al'

It was stated that the word '*Al*-' never changes, although this is not strictly the case. You will be perfectly understood in basic Arabic if you always use '*Al*', but the word can change its form depending on the letter that follows it.

When '*Al*-' is followed by the letters, 'r', 's', 't', 'th', or 'z', then the spelling of '*Al*-' changes – the '*l*' is dropped, and the first letter of the word is doubled to make the pronunciation flow, so e.g. '*al-sayyarah*' (the car) becomes '*as-sayyarah*', '*al-ta'am*' (the food) becomes '*at-ta'am*' and '*al-thaniyah*' (we saw this as 2:00) becomes '*ath-thaniyah*'.

17b. Different Ways of Telling the Time

This is something you can choose to learn or not for yourself, because you can always state the time as shown previously in the Telling the Time section, although native speakers will often use these terms, so it is good to be aware of them.

Basically, Arabic is a little more flexible in this regard than English, in that when we say e.g. 'half past' or 'quarter to' in English, that is about as far as we can go. In Arabic, however, you can add to this, such as 'half and five past' (_:35), or 'five to half past' (_:25), or 'a third and five past' (_:25).

For example,

1:25 can be stated in each of these ways:

'1:00 and 5-and-20'
Al-wahedah wa khamsah wa ishrun
[al wah-heh-dah wah KH'am-sah wah ish-roon]

'1:00 and third-and-5'
Al-wahedah wa tholth wa khamsah
[al wah-heh-dah wah thool'th wah KH'am-sah]

'1:00 and half-minus-5'
Al-wahedah wa nesf ella khamsah
[al wah-heh-dah wah nes-fuh el-lah KH'am-sah]

And,

1:35 is very commonly stated as '1:00 and half and five'
Al-wahedah wa nesf wa khamsah
[al wah-heh-dah wah nes-fuh wah KH'am-sah]

Note that for 1:35, combinations with '*tholth*' ('third) are not really used.

17c. A Note on Arabic Dialects

Arabic is not one simple dialect that everyone understands. In each country or local region where Arabic is spoken, the dialects differ greatly. The Arabic in this book is Modern Standard Arabic (MSA), which was put in place as a bridge between the dialects so that people from different places could communicate and understand each other. This is the most widely understood form of Arabic, and you are best placed learning this if travelling in Arabic-speaking regions, but you should note that people will speak in local dialects when talking to each other. You will naturally pick up vocabulary when you are in each country.

We will give a couple of examples in Egyptian Arabic which, after MSA, is the second most widely understood form (because Egypt is the biggest movie producer, and its movies are popular around the region). Egypt is also the most visited country in the region, so it will be useful to include two or three common differences. So, if you are travelling in Egypt, you might like to note the following.

- Firstly, many words beginning with '*j-*' in MSA begin with a '*g-*' in Egyptian Arabic, e.g.:
beauty *jamal* (MSA); *gamal* (Egy)
good *jayyid* (MSA); *gayyid* (Egy)

- '*mumken*' [moom-ken]. This is a very useful word in Egyptian Arabic, which does not exist in MSA. This word means 'possible', and is used to say, 'Is it possible...?' or 'Can I have...?'
So for example, in Modern Standard Arabic, where you need to ask a full question, e.g. 'Can I have a drink?', there is a full question in Arabic too.

Hal yomkenony tanawol mashroob? (MSA)

But in Egyptian Arabic, all you need is the word '*mumken*' plus whatever it is you are asking for, in this case a drink (*mashroob*):
Mumken mashroob? (Egy)

- '*mish*' [mish]. This is also a common word in Egyptian Arabic, which means 'not', and is used in certain expressions – the most important of these is to say 'want' and 'don't want'. In Egypt, the expression means something like 'not wanting' whereas in Modern Standard Arabic, it is a standard verb and negative. Compare:
I want   *(Ana) la oreed...* (MSA); *(Ana) mish ayez...* (Egy)

Another instance is in the well-used phrase, 'No problem'. In MSA, again, we see the regular negative, '*la*', while in Egyptian Arabic, we see '*mish*'.
No problem   *La moshkelah* (MSA); *Mish moshkelah* (Egy)

17d. Dropping the final '-n' in the verb ending for 'You (plural)' and 'They'.

The example given was:
"**They weren't watching**   *Hum Lam Yakonoon Yoshahedoon*"

The example above is actually incorrect and, in fact, the rule is as follows:
For '**You, plural**' (*Antum*) and '**They**' (*Hum*), when the verb directly follows either '*Lam*' ('didn't') or '*Lan*' ('won't'), the final '-n' of this verb is dropped.

Examples of the dropped final 'n'.

Past Continuous
Hum Lam Yakonoo Yoshahedon
Antum Lam Takonoo Tazhaboon Ela Almadrasa

Past simple
Antum Lam Tazhaboo Ela Almadrasa
Hum Lam Yoshahedoo

Future
Antum Lan Tazhaboo Ela Almadrasa
Hum Lan Yazhaboo Ela Almadrasa

17e. A Note on Word Order

Word order at the beginning of Arabic sentences can differ without changing the meaning of the sentence. This just means that you can begin the sentence with 'noun/pronoun + verb' (e.g. 'I go', 'I do') or 'verb + noun/pronoun' (e.g. 'Go I', 'Do I'), and the meaning stays the same, i.e. this does not make a question, like in English and many other languages.

So this is quite simple, and you may choose to always begin your sentences with the noun or pronoun, but native speakers may use a mxture and it is something you can be aware of. Let's see a few examples:

The car goes fast *Al-sayyarah taseer be-sora'a*
Goes the car fast *Taseer al-sayyarah be-sora'a*

They sold the house *Hum baoo al-manzel*
Sold they the house *Baoo hum al-manzel*

The bus is coming *Al-Bus Ya'atee*
Is coming the bus *Ya'atee Al-Bus*

And that's it – very easy!

18. A Summary of What You Will Need

In essence, this summary is simply reiterating of the most important aspects from the table of contents. Have The intention is to give you a hand in making sure you have enough knowledge and a working vocabulary in Arabic, which is sufficient to manage in the region for an extended period of time, so have a look through, and revisit any of these areas where if you don't feel confident.

- Pronouns – *ana, nahnu, anta, anti, antum, howa, heya, hum*; *-nee/-ee/-y, na, -ka, -ke, -kum, -hu, -ha, -hum*.

- Verbs, including 'to be' & 'to have' + negative (*la*), future (*sa- / lan*). After you gain some experience, you can also cover the past (simple & continuous) and giving orders

- Some common nouns and how to use them, including articles, gender and plurals.

- Some common adjectives and how to use them, **adj** + **noun**, *Al*-**adj** + *al*-**noun**, *Al*-**adj** + **noun, pl. adj** + **pl. noun**

- Other Useful Phrases, including answering questions, modifying, distinguishing, time vocab, location

- Questions & Question Words – *hal, maza, ayna, man, mata, lemaza, kayfa, kam*

- Most Common Questions – Answering these will help you survive many conversations.

- Numbers, including counting, stating how many and how to tell the time.

- Basic Conversation – being able to ask and answer some basic questions.

- Arabic phrases for various situations, including in a taxi, restaurant, bar, coffee shop or retail shop.

19. Also Available

Please visit the <u>Most Basic Languages</u> website (<u>MostBasicLanguages.com</u>), where you will find the things outlined below (please note that if you are an early visitor, this is in the process of being expanded, and more is continually being added if you continue to check back).

Free Resources:
- I am trying to create and offer as many free resources as I can too. This will be notified via an upcoming Facebook page, and many resources will be available on Pinterest (<u>http://pinterest.com/jimmcg1/</u>), which I am just in the process of getting going, including language resources, top restaurants and bars, top travel tips and top schools (for those emigrating), among other things.

Phone Applications:
- At least one FREE app for every language covered. More are being designed and produced to be free.
- Other inexpensive apps designed to bring the easily accessible language of these books (The Most Basic _____).
- Further apps designed to enhance your language learning experience, including exercise books / apps to complement these books, as well as more apps to improve your travel experience.

Travel Apps & Books by Request:
If you have anything you would love to see in an app related to languages, travel or living abroad, or a specialized phrasebook of any kind, then simply send an email to <u>info@mostbasiclanguages.com</u>, and we will aim to have your app or book produced very quickly. It will then be made available cheaply for yourself and others to receive the benefits from.

*** This means that you can have any app or phrasebook you can think of to enhance your travel or language learning experience, within a short time of requesting it. ***

Other books:

- The Most Basic Language Series
All the basics needed to get by in a country, when travelling or living there. This series is being rapidly expanded to include more languages. The books included so far in this series are:
- The Most Basic Chinese – All You Need to Know to Get By
- The Most Basic Japanese – All You Need to Know to Get By
- The Most Basic Lithuanian – All You Need to Know to Get By
- The Most Basic Vietnamese – All You Need to Know to Get By
- The Most Basic Arabic – All You Need to Know to Get By (this book)

- The Most Vital Language Series
This is a series of short e-booklets, outlining days, dates and the vocabulary needed for staying in a hotel, and which I try to make **free** to download on Amazon on the 1st and 15th of each month. The books included so far in this series are:
- The Most Vital Chinese
- The Most Vital Vietnamese

More to come:

- More "**The Most Basic ___**" language books and apps to come. I am currently working with people on a number of other languages to expand the series, as well as converting the series into Android and IOS Applications which will also include the ability to listen to the pronunciation of a native speaker. Please keep an eye out for these in the near future if you are interested.

20. About the Authors

Dr. Ahmad Hamdy

Dr.Ahmad Hamdy is a medical doctor who earned his Bachelor's degree in Medicine and Surgery from Benha University, Egypt, in 2010. He has been working as a freelance translator since 2003, and his clients now include many of the major companies and bodies in the world.

He is certified as 'pro' level in English to Arabic and Arabic to English translation, and was selected by the very popular Proz.com translators' workplace portal to be the leader of the Proz.com "Arabic localization team". He has handled work for many governmental agencies in the US and Western Europe, as well as many international organizations.

Dr.Ahmad has always had a passion for Arabic, and he is also a poet and writer. He has tried, with Jim McGlasson, to simplify the Arabic language as much as possible in this book, in a way that is very easy to understand. If you are in need of quality Arabic translations, please send your request to Dr.Ahmad's email address: scrptlancer@yahoo.com.

You can also check Dr.Ahmad's professional web-based profile at: http://www.proz.com/profile/1309414.

We hope you enjoy our book and would be more than happy to receive your comments and views about it.

Jim McGlasson

You can read a little about Jim's background and motivation in writing these books at www.MostBasicLanguages.com.

21. Final Note

The Middle East covers a large area and takes in many countries, each with their own culture and identity. Despite some media portrayals in the West, the people can be some of the friendliest and most welcoming anywhere in the world, and it is a wonderful region to travel around, meet people and see some wonderful sights, both man-made and natural.

If you make the effort to learn the language presented in this book, you will have a vastly improved travel experience, as goes for travelling anywhere armed with a bit of the language. You will be able to meet and chat to locals, who very much appreciate hearing visitors making the effort to speak their language, as well as finding yourself being in a much better position with bargaining for prices.

So make the effort to learn this little bit, and you will find your trip is greatly enhanced.

11394015R00047

Printed in Great Britain
by Amazon.co.uk, Ltd.,
Marston Gate.